I0807592

Lives

Lucas Hunt

Vagabond Press
~ out there but hard to find ~

Published by
Vagabond Press

© 2006 Lucas Hunt

All rights reserved

First Edition
Printed in the United States of America

Library of Congress Control Number 2006920333
ISBN-10 0-9755716-2-1
ISBN-13 978-0-9755716-2-0

Vagabond Press
P.O. Box 4830
Austin, TX 78765
vagabondpress.com

Vagabond Press ~

Here it is! I am confident of the quality of this aesthetic adventure. My heart and humor are in it like never before; it is a mix of what I feel and know to be good plus imagine true. It may be helpful to read my work with the philosophical spirit in mind and to think illusion necessary for understanding. Although I do not oppose the idea of nothingness as primary condition or basic reality, I do believe art is a willingness to come out of that sacred circle, if only to give an instant of recognition or perhaps to represent the diverse manifestations of nothing. I can not be completely atheistic because of this faith; that human action is directly responsible for earthly fortunes, that fate is in our hands even though we often strive with meaningless despair and the impulse towards immortal works and souls. Passion has long been the food of my endeavors to express some bit of existence accurately and with illusion in mind. I continue to match dream with the objective world in hope of better perceiving life through ordinary yet profound senses. My hopes are high yet this is my umpteenth collection of poetry, all distinct in theme and style, so that everything is tempered by a dramatic insignificance that lets me simultaneously laugh as I struggle to reach ever distant pinnacles of joy.

Sincerely yours,
Lucas Hunt

CONTENTS

To Sarah and Simon

Lives

Lucas Hunt

Invocation

Of origins beyond explanation,
ruled by laws unknown,
Come spirit of poetry, muse,
sing us something new!

Prepare for Nothing

No more meaningful experience exists than one
we can't fully apprehend,
One that arrives entire, unexpected, mature—
And reminds us both of birth and death
Through acts that appear to transform reality,
turning it auspicious.

Explain your emptiness, oh grand agitator,
When days are just a circuitous search to accrue
And night an elemental battle to maintain!

Protect us from gloom inherent in inquiry,
thy hateful occurrence,
Let us not search the skies to be convinced,
For here we have the practical glory
To imagine what's beyond the stars.

Works of genius convey ample evidence,
Their aura spreads subliminal proceeds;
We must bare change and endure despair—
The ability to understand has limitations.

I Am the Poet

I.

I am the poet who stays suffering,
Who works and wonders about all that ever was,
        what is now, what will be.

I hear the voices of people cry out for change,
The history of struggle means more than we think,
        today it is relevant.
The present world is not just,
Future populations gasp in horror at what occurs,
A process of labor and reward exploits those
Who do not own the products of their toil,
Who give freely to those they love,
Who face destruction by force,
Whose laughter is immortal as their sacrifice.

Heroes and villains
Everywhere, spread across the globe,
In the atmosphere, unconscious
Beings capable of extraordinary feats!

There is nothing left to sell, no more to advertise,
What comes now is greater than we imagined,
A change in the chemistry of space,
An event that defies rational explanation
        becomes common news.
We will discover it soon with the microscope
        and through the telescope,
An army of miracles comprises us,
The fiber, tube, knot and cord of the universe,
        these quirks enlarge us.

We absolute animals of flesh
Participate in puzzling equations,
The apparent order of things is illusory
    and there is more,
The layers are many, the well deep, the core
    only the initiation,
The part we play in the old graphic drama,
    our miniscule scenes,
The tremendous vibration of blood that rocks
    then steals away,
That none are too deaf to hear nor any
    able to counterfeit,
Though one day we may get it.

Hear, listen to this natural rhythm,
Does it ask you to propagate revolution,
Does it tell you to take a different path?

I serve the human function,
My poems correspond to the motions of planets,
Host abstract potential and philanthropic ends,
    are not immune to evil
But beat the drum of love before war,
Seek no glory in death rather adulate life itself,
Maintain the right to breathe, eat, drink, fornicate
    and verbalize exaltation.

II.

Oh renewal! Fill your words with powerful current
    and let the crooked tide flow
Into surf, pass into sea born energy unbound,
Gather momentum and spread spirit on the water
    of this sleeping harbor!
Oh watery undulation, bury me in your nucleus,
Swallow this superficial song and vomit up
    something greater yet!

Address to the Party

To start with, love flourished
in green fields naive,
focused on formless details,
provided its existence
grew enlightened to decay.

And some stayed, eventually
the heartache arrived;
in smoke, ennui and abuse
our childhood expires
and naturally revolt occurs.

For the dynamic freedom
necessary to take risks,
deceit first broke the rule
reason would not obey,
thought untangled speech.

If none longer leapt at void,
men and women could
confront this more clearly;
student, artist, athlete—
all love to flee authority.

Imagine a weapon that will
rebuild footing, life ruins,
master preparing for wars,
find the nerve and humor
to learn instruments, curse.

Live like a beautiful savage,
a terrific sphinx of sex,
scream at temporal plans,
work in commodity markets
to defend, negotiate, earn.

One Moment of Realization

Solace in the fact of new generations, wisdom of youth,
    somehow they'll manage
To navigate this contradictory domain,
Years from now lead original exploration,
Evolve paradigm of the universe,
Discover cures for disease, crime and war,
Design tools to satisfy every need and succeed
    in making empathetic men.

An empirical utopia is absurd
Though experiments inform us, suggest how all began
    and how we might stave off the end.

Must the world be destroyed, cataclysm disintegrate
    our biblical refuge once more,
Have men seen it all, parks and fields go,
Lots and buildings emptied, life liquidated?

No, another trillion years of tedium will not do,
    of adaptation and migration,
This stage would take forever to replicate.

We could sustain the planet, concentrate energy
    to preserve equilibrium
Between nations, nature, races, weather and machines
Then balance a credulous look in our eyes,
    one of actual faith.

The Beached Whale

It lay there vacant eyed,
Sixty-six feet of mammalian demigod for all to ogle,
Spouting saline geysers no longer,
Tongue protruding out enormous slack jaw,
A once colossal grace gone motionless.

The large crowd gathers round its alien cadaver
    with cameras silent,
Eager to take it all in, unsure exactly how,
None have seen a bigger beast in suit of flesh.

It lay on the grand scale where
Myth grows realistic and divinity dissolves,
The single being that outweighs all others, deceased.

Hesitant to arrive at partial conclusion,
Apt to want the full story, people curiously circle,
Unable to resist an enormous speculation,
    life's eventual end!

Undeniable imagery,
Could this not all be mirage?

One asked a uniformed man guarding the carcass
    if it were palpable
And received no for an answer,
Then they asked what authority this man had
To keep people from touching things
    and were shown a gun.

Is power a joke,
For who could shoot a five-year-old for trying
    to get close enough to feel,
To put an innocent finger upon the truth,
Why teach that child the latest definition of crime?

Unorthodox Legendry

Ugh, must we earn ourselves to death as well,
    race against machine,
Compete at self-destruction for approval
Or do as inner voices tell us to,
Secure enough, then split, with what's left
    of sanity and health?

Damn it John Henry,
You compromise the fundaments of life,
    body and brain
For vainglorious reasons, while man
Is adequate before the fact, noble upon birth,
Only needs minimal things to become
    more like his god.

For instance: aphrodisiac distillates of air,
        the spiritual liquid water,
        delectable nourishment food,
        warm matrimonial women,
        an assuring universe of stars.

Why the long day,
Don't you love your life,
Must a master's pleasure come first,
Do you like the work of a soul-selling slave?

Enjoy it now, appreciate today, know we cheat
    the laborer well,
And John, fight exploitation!
As for eventual mortality, don't worry
            I assure you it is nothing.

Prayer for Idiots

Who foregoes fun because they perceive some serious
business occurring elsewhere
Are too sober for the world, unfortunately, fools.

For it takes courage to carouse, to get famously drunk,
Command an empire of imaginary significance,
Roam the streets of town and city like a dog or cat,
Urinate in puddle and alley, off bridge and platform,
howl at the moon in rapture.

Dare to enter an endless party, seek revolving door
to apartment, house, hall, loft
Basement, bedroom, garage and lounge
To map the gamut of experience in conversation,
joke, parody, sing, confess
Over wine, whiskey, beer, brandy, smoke
And casual introduction, eager reunion—
Trace the dreamlike flow of steps up and down stairs
into taxicab and out of airplane,
Bathe in the cheer of club, crowd and television,
live band, jukebox, holiday
Church and state celebrations for fun,
Just ordinary nights when friends stop by to visit,
Reminisce, regret, cuss—it's never too late to dream.

But be careful how you worship,
When you find yourself at the gates, whichever ones,
warnings will be worthless
And the preacher was right, for all your studies
will then be useless.

Go without logic or reason, poor weapons
Against an insoluble enigma that tempts us to try
And take truth; enjoy the dying hours of youth, be brave!

To My Mistress

If you do not exist I will invent you,
        meet with no one,
Look at air with affection and hold
        an imaginary hand.

I will dream of being with you now
        just for inspiration,
And stop believing in eventual us,
        dismiss the desire.

If you do not exist I will abandon
        the world of reality,
Fake your face, your voice, your
        warm naked body.

And make believe how you quiver
        with real pleasure
In your eyes, on your lips, the loll
        of your soft breast.

Ah well, the world is too practical
        for our fantasies,
If only they were physical and here,
        this ache no more.

For you torment and encourage me
        to take life itself,
Thus love enjoys greater transport
        than ever before.

What the Sea Stole

Hold tide, hold your copious motions for a minute
While I replay this summer tragedy for
All to seize the danger inherent—
Days begin alike until something changes.

Families gather for weekend picnics on the beach,
        friends sunbathe and swim,
The wind picks up then settles down as children
        run rampant on the sand;
People like to party their days off,
Water makes life bearable for local and tourist
Where land leaves them disappointed.

It is freedom they seek, those surfers who brave
        sharks and squalls to ride,
Who mount the equine wavery, harness wild
        fluid power on boards
And heel the breaking thrust of gravity.

Others enjoy the calm solitude of a long walk
        on sunlit shores,
They envision a gilded ocean surface
And soak in dreamy leisure, entranced by gulls
That float so guilelessly above the human crowd,
        ready to dip down for handouts
Or invade an empty blanket,
Screaming with laughter all the while.

Young women wear the least amount of clothes,
Their diminutive suits cover, to great effect,
        burgeoning spheres,
It is hard not to look or look away,
Nature construes to keep eyes glued on beauty;
Whether lust or fascination with female pleasure,
The loveliness of grown up girls is paramount,
        it puts life in a peaceful bed
Rather than at war and dead.

The aged have their wrinkles and one day I will too,
They sit content in lawn chairs under the sun
        watching their grandkids,
And those in shape are still attractive too.

Of course what we hide matters most,
Personality takes the pageant, choose character,
A sort of soul inside the body better represents it.

Now let us pretend a man has the freedom to elect
        a mate and even honesty,
Will he fasten to one who awes his eye the most,
And will they be the same to own his heart?
Love is irrational jewelry we cling to without logic.

Let's return to our equally romantic coastal scene;
Couples lay quiet, sometimes talk, genuinely serene,
A volleyball game starts, radios echo off umbrellas,
The salty odor of ocean pervades the fresh air
As several people stare out across the bright water
        with curious faces,
Shielding their eyes with hand-shaped visors.

A call is made to two young boys gone out too far
        from shore, they are brothers
And best friends, more, they drift apart.

A louder, more urgent, second call,
A lone surfer grabs his board, sprints to the water
        and swims with speed,
He has to reach the two young boys.

The third call is a cry, somebody help them, hurry,
A terrible anxiety sweeps the beach,
Only one conversation takes place, some rush
        to phone for help
Others wade out only to discover
Too great a distance, too turbulent a sea.

A cruel tide has carried the brothers apart,
Now one slips away from the other
And drifts much farther out.

A fourth call, who makes it? boats and helicopters
are on the way,
The lone surfer closes in on the nearest boy,
Can't see the other, only hears
"Where is he, where is my brother?"

Now all life is in peril, the surfer paddles
Back to shore with what little strength he has left,
The boy he has saved cries loud and louder.

Grown men and women, fathers and mothers themselves,
now openly weep, hysteria overcomes,
They have witnessed some of the worst in their lives
But this is too much, yet only the beginning,
When the surfer returns exhausted, heroic, with
the boy whom none can silence,
Not now nor ever, to the wave-broken beach,
He just screams inconsolable, "my brother is dead!"

It is true, no humor can make it false,
That too young boys once went for a swim
And even after extensive search, only one survived.

Haiku

Winter cardinals
fly from field to tree;
droplets of blood, sparks of spring.

North Fork Afternoons

In an epoch ripe for ceremony
  thirsty adults gather to taste
various wines at vineyards
  ideal for literary readings.

With nose and tongue select
  diverse distillation of grape
for subtle flavor and bouquet,
  perhaps to string quartets.

They lounge on sunlit patio
  with bottles of chilled white;
some sweet, others dry, and
  chat with old acquaintance.

Then soft cheese and cherries,
  rosemary-encrusted bread,
almonds, avocado, chocolates
  followed by chicory coffee.

After naps ride to the sound
  and watch the water heave,
or take gentle strokes offshore,
  casually surface to breathe.

It is a treat to live out east
  on heaven's isle, tomorrow
comes quite regularly, time
  passes within an eye's wink.

Woman on the Shore

She spoke the word, the name, the symbol and knew
    the bitter joy it brought,
She was that which unknowingly represents
Another and yet outshines the original,
Her voice more powerful, person undeniable.

Mother, called her daughter, love, her husband
    yet she heard them not,
For her eyes were fastened to mine
And we were one, strangers to each other,
A woman on the shore and I, totally unacquainted,
Joined in a mysterious agreement.

Come on, said her daughter, let's go, her husband
    yet she moved not,
Rather stood and stared directly at me,
Hypnotized, unconcerned, possessed.

Again the word, the name, the symbol that she read
    on my face, saw inside me
And spoke aloud, in a gentle whisper,
An expression near apology.

She stayed, did not leave when her family called,
    did not move an arm,
She stood there still, perfect, until
They stopped what they were doing to watch,
Waiting, wondering what had happened,
    what would happen.

Then I felt too much, that it was time for her to go,
    told her so with my eyes
And thanked her, gasped as she turned away,
    held back trembling
As the waves crashed into my ears.

City Sirens

Yell, yell at those unwilling to refrain
 from all consuming industry,
Laugh at human enterprise, the crawl
Up frank elevation toward lofty summit,
That dear old urge to leave behind a legacy.

Robbers and thieves, be generous
To those of us who like to cultivate gardens,
Send an airplane ticket now and then
And reduce the fines the poor have to pay,
For as we travel this glorious country
 in search of happiness
There is not much extra cash to go around
And it would help to be lenient.

Loudly they wail, calling us to the streets
 even as they alarm,
Not unlike some temptress buildings
 full of able bodies,
Muscular men and voluptuous women,
The same implements as in war only minds
 aimed at making money,
Some faithful others complete infidels,
Creatures of dignity, lust and improvisation,
Beings with ritual and responsibility,
Earnest, ironic, dull, mercurial, fastidious
 and essential to each other—

What for, to rear exceptionally fair people,
 a just human society,
To piece the broken globe back together,
Direct weaker links to unite their strengths
And separate sex drives from ambulance beds.

To My Father

I owe it to the man—
Who made me out of nothing to grow under the sun,
Who baptized me in rustic weather, provided food
    to eat and water to drink,
Who spoke me words, rhymes to inspire,
The spirit that sustains my every exploration.

Who knows in depth—
About wells, foundation, plumbing and thermodynamics,
About electricity, lumber, gas, mechanics,
    the concrete of family
About neighbors, relatives and old friends,
The wind as it whistles through the pines.

About autumnal things—
How days end sooner and melancholy sometimes sets,
How hillsides go from green to yellow, orange, red
    and the harvest begins,
How grasshoppers fiddle and bullfrogs croak,
The ritual of natural joy enriches each evening.

Establish the Future

In an era rife with commentary and friction
Who cares whether experiment or nature
　　　　alter perception first,
Either way, chemicals intoxicate
And familiar streets appear unique.

To say something new can come of crisis,
To operate a vehicle high or imagine
　　　　aircraft into skyscraper
Demolishes paradigm; it took old
Cavaliers of consciousness to conceive
Of digital and cellular media,
A surge of invention, video, satellite,
　　　　astronomical difference—
All there before, latent in the framework.

To guess what lucrative trade is next
Visionaries access all cognition
And now and then partake;

　　　　to yield to ancient currents,
　　　　drown in everyday stream,
　　　　trek submerged mountain,
　　　　prophesy hypnotic lengths.

Ample amounts of metamorphic substance
　　　　accumulate before us,
Inexhaustible supply, potential raises,
Vast wealth develops innovation galore,
　　　　a visible variety.

Mavericks deviate,
Laws that block creation are not for them,
　　　　they dynamite obstacle,
Draw complimentary cash from banks,
　　　　enter any premises,
Pharmacies full of magazines and drugs,
And take whatever is necessary—
For them all shops are open.

To radically change the way we look at things,
abolish every norm,
Oxygen demands such variation;
Heirs to revolt, here's invite to proceed.

Catharsis

Numerous times I have tried
to say something in vain;
Now thunder diminishes and
rain yields way to ribbon.

The Muse of Bitterness

Devious, I will not blaze about your inferno nor
use paranoid language
To lay conspiracy on your breast,
Rather gratitude for initiating me.

Why purchase imposition?
It's all beautiful lies, meat and mechanics,
the supple energy coursing,
Layers of superstition and under them a monster
whose every move is ancient calculus,
Who triumphs over and over and over.

Once sweet rituals excited
Now a fatal grace extinguishes passing time
And nothing profound happens to keep us
from fading away.

It is only our spirits that forge justification
up, ahead, back
Through drama and boredom again.

That's why some call you cold others vain
or just cruel bitch,
Because your beauty torments them and your
power sabotages.

Moving Rock

Apparently some sculptors inaccurately fashion
abstractions of the world
And their work, if it can be called work,
Does nothing to further dialogue or inspire people
To live different, if not greater lives.

Such sham chiselers don't deserve the attention
They who create masterful sculpture do,
Whose art occupies a space in the imagination
many have accessed.

Picture if you can, curved geometric figures
Dance through trees onto yards and bend
To drink from fountain and pond.

The true architecture of their image supposed,
Metal intimations of more fluid nature,
Bronze and stainless steel allegories welded
To reflect eye's metamorphic light,
Dream material carved in solid beam,
polished linear magic.

Others heat and twist wood,
chainsaw ice or stump,
some throw clay then fire
in kilns for pottery.

There are myriad elements to mold,
from gem to bone to gold,
But the best, subject of this poem,
is stone, common stone.

Yet the good stuff is hard to get, must be mined
or personally found, bought
Or shipped from far and that ain't cheap,
Can cost more than sculptures sell for.

I met a tall man, one physical titan,
Who smoothed rough edged rock into spherical
Forms that sit well on tables or stand out in a corner.

His philosophy, expounded in the beginning,
Translates to action and involvement,
For in order to continually craft the stone
    he needs a steady supply,
As of yesterday the rock came to him,
But tomorrow he will go to the rock.

Thus, in order to get sufficient amounts of stone
He left town, and in moving bequeathed some
I and another lifted with crane onto truck,
    to haul to another studio.

    So it was that moving rock
    became much more than
    just shifting some boulders
    from one place to another.

Rather, inheriting the wisdom,
That a time may come when it's necessary to cease
    waiting for it to come,
When one must also go to the source.

On Overcoming Confusion

One event appears more useful than others:
ejaculate before chaos, direct pressure,
go from gradual violence to organic whole,
formal system, clandestine juggernaut,
that wild exclamation of individual energy,
compel, explode, sublimate and repeat.

At Night They Play

Long hours of work are hard for sure
weigh heavy on skin and bone;
when human grace can not endure
the burden is overthrown.

Here gather women, children, men and pet
to enjoy recreation's calm effect
because our population grows with stress
all crowd the park for leisure, nature soothes
and games of ease relax exhausted folk;
the working class depends upon its back
yet somehow manages to find the strength
to go on, to stand up and demonstrate.

Easy weather, do not rain this evening,
sports are scheduled, people count on inning,
half and match to rouse their weary spirits
to athletic feats—do revive from
daily struggle with miraculous pitch,
kick and swing in front of family or
casual spectator, thus have mercy,
let no storm delay communal gathering.

Fun calls the cult of exercise to feed,
to go outside and run around;
without the freedom of movement
would riot in every town.

Portrait of A Hobo

With a stick raw at one end from the breaking
propped on his shoulder,
black garbage bag knotted round it,
he strode along the narrow edge of highway
with knowing smile:

"I am a hobo, this my symbol.
Each morning, while most drive to work,
I begin the long journey that is my occupation
down smoggy roads.

By lunchtime I am famished from walking
and seek the shade of tree or bridge.
Sometimes I beg for food others purchase
and give to me generously.
Other times I spend money I have made
doing various jobs;
digging, building, cleaning, whatever.

I don't mind work but prefer the freedom
of long morning walks
and afternoons of rest
by country rivers or in city parks.
The public disapproves but secretly
wishes to be free;
free from work and cares,
from mortgage and monthly payment,
committees and team,
license, contract, agreement
(mine is with time and the good Lord)
files, form, membership, meeting,
loan, rent, budget, bill and obligation.

Like I said,
my day begins with exercise until weather
and hunger slow me down,
after that I don't do much but lounge around.

Once in a while I hop a train, yes, we still do
          hitch a ride or take a bus
to visit people, several times
I've crossed this great land to attend
          a friend's funeral.
And then there are wine and stories,
that ongoing party with a big bonfire
          in the woods,
with beans and franks, strong whiskey—
some play fiddle, banjo, harmonica
and we sing old railroad songs
and yell and laugh and cry
for family or comrades,
until the stars lull us to sleep.

Although I look alone
I'm not, there are many others like me,
some still go about normal lives
others I meet impromptu and we joke
          about the punctual world,
how it dismisses our existence as aimless
          and fails to see the irony,
how it uses then abandons whatever it wants.

Generally, we are grateful for our lots,
for the chance to travel the world,
free to explore it awhile.

Maquoketa Caves

Crawled out cold, dark, wet labyrinth, a hole in the earth,
  mud puddle, grabbed the gnarled roots of trees,
  kicked at ferns and spider webs
And saw farther in the night sky than ever before.

We laughed to live, to breathe the air, to see
  the planets stand above us,
Because the deepest cave is a deadly closet
And it's not easy to slide through rocky tubes
  with little light on hand,
Nor face the possibility of accidental entombment,
Of being trapped in a remote recess, a tight nowhere
  where screaming goes unheard.

But to explore a palace underground, to enter a world
  few have ever imagined,
To pass through threshold, cross out fear,
To break terror's hold on body and mind
  and transgress limitation.

A salute to spelunkers,
Yeh, spelunkers, whose courage seems insane yet there
  be virgin territory, subterranean adventure
For inverted voyagers, worms of truth.

What else lies below the globe's thin surface,
  more eludes our appreciation,
What ancient wisdom buried in the dirt,
What secrets suffocate in hidden enclosure,
What medicine yet to be found, history discovered,
  species named, civilizations reborn,
Music transcribed, poetry, plants, beads, dishes,
  idiosyncratic tool, sculpture, bones,
  jewelry, clothes, plaything, key?

One imagines the story artifacts tell
And for those who delve into forbidden zones
  in search of something priceless,
Who formulate curiosity and follow,
Life is worth more than it was before having risked it.

The Close Followers

It takes a nation bent on home repair
and self improvement to destroy
abusive tyranny. Behold the plan:
to liberate the human race

from ignoble government.
Amid both corruption and disorder
democracy won decisive wars,
now people have the power

and reserve the right to select
leadership from all society.
Anyone can become the president,
every citizen has a vote

and driven, will determine more;
to make romantic history
before the iron gates of death.
The outcome of this world is definite.

Crime Up the Street

Murder, approximate deities, and rape
left an insane effigy by the road;
automobile torched.

Now no tender sleep,
the basis quakes, obsidian erupts
and mad midnight nightmares awake.

Snowplow thunder scrapes
blood from shrine, nothing less, run
to a vigil that devastates sense.

Justice appoints guilt
and acquits the innocent, here
twenty-two years to life in prison.

Absurd sentence, no interlude of time
could serve as resurrection or
undo acidic tears.

Who heals from death
only to die again, oh implausible ones,
defy the rules, grant peace.

Why Summer Remains

Cheers for love, athletic season, love once felt
    forevermore and left
A lone fountain to scale the deluge rain,
Does uplift and elevate horizon,
Single jet against the rest, memory made.

Still the candle rises
Amid talk at tables set for reception,
For couples standing outside museum and hall
With dinner plans in stylish dress,
Where evening crowds salute the sunset
    with glasses full of joy.

A toast to absent guests, celebrated friends,
They may have climbed stairs and leapt
    off laughter's rooftop,
Their existence may be conjecture
However, we scan identical sets of stars
And equally indicate night for ceremony.

Behold, examples of faith appear invisible
    yet are demonstrable,
The steady eye of tomorrow glares
At points beyond perimeter,
Abstractions essayed in summer,
Seawater splashing in the air unattached,
Lit mist saturates our vision with abundant
    darkness and excess,
The reason is obscure to one involved—

Do you sense a slow departure,
Ascent to higher, less impermanent, positions
Or significance in steady change,
As one passes through permutation's door;

How once wounded, it arrives
To stretch a second into eternities of flight?

Poem of Protest

Some men say war is our story and blood
makes rich fields; it leaves widows and kids
without parents and people without limbs.

War takes away, destroys faith in humanity,
lessens, breaks and traumatizes the spirit
of love that is kind, that listens to grievance.

Men are rude machines that kill one another
with religious assault, with sick deception,
whatever it takes to win a corporeal fight.

Life would be ridiculous if I did not know
there are some who actually wish to hurt,
who lust to shower red blood on the fields.

Where will I grow my crops when the army
comes to smash skulls into the brown dirt,
where is the brother I lost, my only brother?

Stare at the Sun

A jealous impulse steals,
To stare at the sun, drink directly from river,
        eat mud, strip off clothes
Then fire-eyed, throw up polluted water,
Defecate earth and pass out naked.

                Stark and vulnerable,
To face a void others have,
Stand in defiance of natural law
And without internal reason, set the record
        for survival.

Visions and clamorous voices come;
Many are in need of immediate attention,
        affordable medicine,
Overdose, gunshot wound, patients
Disconnected from ordinary interaction,
The mad, starving, impoverished, diseased-
        all sequestered
According to degree of contagion.

Plus, items take imaginary meaning, vehicles
        turn into monsters,
Statues move that should be still,
Little is stable, details do not hold
And solid goes liquid till illusions expose
A parallel fabric in the universe.

                It's white out,
There is growing whiteness in the atmosphere,
Light, holy light, complete whiteness.

Vision of Birth

That power which is beyond our ability to control,
beyond comprehension,
Reveals fragments of the future to us whole
And leaves no real understanding why—
We suffer tremendously the gift.

While inside a bar, dashing through the doorway
before turning on the light
An ephemeral episode came,
Superseded ordinary objects; sink, wall, toilet—
An injurious beauty conceived.

A woman and child in a metropolitan park;
The mother bent over a stroller, lovely, brunette
lifting a baby to her bosom,
The daughter bright, her countenance spry,
Set on new legs just able to stand
To the delight of both, a perfect couple.

If that hallucination comes true
It will demonstrate the plainness of compression,
the way of projection,
That there is more than we can relay.

Psychic altitudes, ecstatic possibility,
The roots of madness propose interpretation
And condescend to make a meaning or a myth
of transcendental experience.

We sometimes see flesh rot on bone
Or find fascinating armageddon.

Dare you chastise those who wander through time
with prophetic content,
Born to the reality of supernatural bodies?

Clear Visitations

I.

We look in books for answers to the question life
 and find many there,
More, beyond the lines, importance—
Few get to know their worth in time,
It visits us spontaneous and leaves without a word.

Still more, there is no name for what one cannot
 put a physical finger on,
It is unknowable, overwhelms, a power
Rarely tapped, less often pumped, never cupped
That makes our cerebrum seem like cracked utensil.

II.

The greatest pleasure lies in touching one another,
 even in splendid solitude,
For the person who strives alone is not—
Rather encompassed by bands of casual entities,
Instigates contact between unlikely agents
And forms acquaintance where none thrived before.

Who are you cordial angels, familiar guides
That engineer each article from scratch
And administer instant inspiration?

III.

Traces of greatness continue to exalt our endeavor
 to improve the world,
Transmit euphoria and coronary tremor—
Assemble interests in order to acquire
A foreign faculty that assimilates every argument.

A real cyclorama lures me to swell this relation
 till the fit passes,
What comes from miscellaneous means
And leaves new circumstances to be weighed,
Ingenious spirits are like alien morsels to digest.

Refugees

Behold the residue of some military commotion,
Violence echoes off tents, people cry against
an endless barrage of night,
One gives birth another gets beaten to death,
The powerless poor driven from their land
by soldiers with guns
Now without shelter, food, clothes or water.

An entire generation of sick homeless children;
They do not ride to school in buses and cars,
They do not learn to read and write words
in their language,
Their education consists of plain suffering,
Their contribution to the world is lost.

One woman weeps, her husband was executed
for no apparent reason,
No government maintains power
Only lawless men who use brutal force
to cause some to bow
Others to resist with equal determination
And some to remain unmoved.

Laughter from the perimeter, a small symposium
has gathered tonight
To play cards and share from a bottle,
Their talk is of days past and things to come,
of impractical undertakings,
One of them has become a prostitute,
Away from camp, they take turns on a blanket.

A guerilla unit has already organized to resist
the illegal occupation,
Young and old form into squadrons,
They will leave this very night to confer
with neighbors,
Soon a full scale rebellion will take place,
It will be crushed by the invading troops,
Many native people will die as a result.

The foreigners sleep safe in their barracks.
They dream of their families back home,
Of holiday gatherings, pets, and peace.

There are no kitchens, no hospitals, no churches
Humanitarian relief can not reach the area,
Many will perish if help does not come,
Some will commit suicide out of despair.

Others lay crippled by an outbreak of influenza,
            feverish amid flies and excrement,
Those not afflicted by disease are restless,
            waiting to return home,
Unaware they will never go back,
Unaware those who survive will be resettled.

To My Grandfather

He communes with mountain,
  mind upon their peaks,
Enshrined in Appalachia,
  forever told to speak.

A Telepathic Device

People developed technology to project unconscious
content onto screens—
By holding an alloyed lever that senses feeling
thought, memory and dream,
We can conjure mental imagery.

This machine divines the mind, provides new
methods for treatment
And can measure madness through the film
of quick deception.

It translates psyche into simultaneous picture
By turning an inward eye upon the self,
shows cinematic readings of the soul.

The power to observe abnormal
or sane brain functioning,
To record imagination on chips
or present the ineffable!

To communicate without language,
With eyes closed and expression in hand,
Focus on something or nothing in particular
Until inner visions transmit external revelations.

The Business of Squirrels

The saga of my yard is based on the presence of a dozen
furry maniacs; there are crows,
An idiot on a lawnmower polluting the environment,
The rotted leftovers of one hundred refrigerators
thrown out for compost
And an occasional migrant taking a shortcut,
Yet the most interesting action is the acrobatics
of these strange rodents.

Sometimes I wonder if this is the local insane asylum
for the squirrel kingdom,
Their version of a hospital for the psychotic.
Then I observed others in the neighborhood
And traveled to different towns, to the countryside
In hopes of spotting one stable squirrel, yet saw none.
To the contrary, my studies find these cute little animals
mentally abnormal,
To be clear—they revel in perilous situations.

A squirrel will sprint the length of a tall tree limb and leap
without the slightest hesitation
Toward no specific landing pad.
It will then grasp whatever branch comes
to the grip of its paw,
Swing like a monkey, twitter, cluck, bark
And recently I heard one attempt a rooster's crow.

What causes a critter to be so frantic?
It's well known squirrels feast on shelled meat,
which may explain them,
For when they are not mating they seek it constantly,
And that it's hard to find may account for their loss
of emotional control,
It is possible raw hunger ravages their minds,
That squirrels are monomaniacal for nuts.

Watching them play, one notes a highly excitable nature
        during social interaction,
That the animal is compelled to give chase
For sport or out of territorial aggression,
Either way, squirrels cause unforgettable displays;
They wrestle, box, tackle, and pounce on one another for fun.

To sum up their behavior, squirrels are often nervous,
        regularly dart behind trees,
Have paranoid dispositions, are unpredictable,
Indifferent to the danger of climbing telephone poles,
Enjoy risky stunts on power lines for recreation,
        and are most industrious
In matters of their own imagination.

Miami Beach

When a poet is on the beach
he hears the sound of creation
and loves what the universe
has made for him, also,
he gives to those who want
the object of their desire,
so that they call him god.

It Comes as a Relief

Some pronounce it bliss, others a kind of curse,
those who deny it is useful at all say
'knowledge is better than none' yet what good
is that when we can not forget
            a haunting experience?

            The hair of a brunette
washes her face, lightning looms in her eye,
the flex of her neck, she slowly sighs yes,
taste of her breast, aroma in her thighs,
the motion of her hips mimics god.

            Perhaps we will not
recall the true innocence of our beginnings
but what is better, there is always desire
and memory has more than ignorance,
for they who choose it consummate life.

Ah Autocide!

Life without love is unbearable
and I would rather hang from beam
or pour blood from both wrists,
stare down shotgun, toe on trigger
or dine on an overdose of pills.

It is not worth living
and self examination endless,
so go, go, go to bed
and dream, dream of death.

With cliffs for pillows
pain's finale will be stupendous.

Recall, birth introduces us
to suffering's habitude,
fate decides whether we smile
or scoff at another day;
to wake, shower, shave, dress
for work, for struggle.

And sex, intense experience,
shudder under another's tongue
braced for orgasmic seizure,
feel the flood of climax come.

Forsake those intermittent flashes
    of unpredictable yes,
affirming jolts of nervous energy,
like a pinch of manic foresight,
    obsession's impulse

Before you do heinous cancellation,
Spuriously resign, ah autocide,
call out if you can, call out for
another day, additional hours
    of disintegrating time.

Leave what isn't yours alone,
death will come on its own,
what's written will be read
aloud, wait, wait for me.

To My Wife

You are not mute but have the power
to give the world back to itself,
to bring life back to life.
You are a calm, sentient voice,
an elegant arrangement;
remedy, satiation, catch.

Love Is All, Let Go

How it changes,
fashions the soul a ceremonial receptacle,
molds dreams into self-fulfilling shape,
concentrates chaos in units of sense,
asks the mystery to produce.

It guides blood through cryptic passage
and delivers being from boredom.

And modifies occupation for the better,
charges us to enjoy this world;
makes a birth of morning, death of night,
converts day to miniature life.

Love is total possession, be sure,
it is nothing without madness and ends
          in tragic transformation.

Yet how many misread the sign that says
          'lane change ahead,'
interpret it instead as 'love changes us,'
thus make truth a joke and terminate
all judgment save that of the heart.

It lets us to escape reincarnation's wheel
and the cyclical pattern of history.

Also inspires good deeds, negates evil,
confirms one and all religious,
refers us to selflessness.

Love is no tyrant to obey,
No fascist emotion to which we succumb,
Rather, it is all, life nothing.

Poem of God

I.

As the sun astonishes our intellect, its intensity too great for language,
So the magnitude of history exceeds our ability to understand truth.
Thus we must become agnostic again, to appreciate the origins
Of consciousness and change our errant course.

Life is conducive to much, especially creation, agonizing over itself
Till fruit are born of a universal tree and rich aromas spread
Across the galaxy—existence comes slowly, nourishes the eternal
And ever patient, not nature but the actual pace of planets,
Everything still far amid the stars.

The gift of earth remains unseen, none have walked or even crawled
Out the first recess yet a watery globe pervades, whether found
Or discovered, it includes infinite accumulations of fortune.

II.

Yes, we are born anomalies, not even close to being ourselves yet,
Decillions of light-years away from appearance, an unthinkable play,
Our place a mere mass of dark dismal stuff primary to everything;
Inequality advancing out of indistinguishable nothing; brine, womb
Teeming multitudes of fluent energy amalgamating a storm of seed.

I am sure there is chaos, thunder, quake, crash, a furious overture
Of primeval instruments blasting symphonies of dust and fire,
Bubble boiling volcanic explosions, black smoke, red clouds,
Yellow rivers, deserts and massive ice mountains gash the surface
With sharp steel blades, glass boulders break, loud screeching
And gaseous fumes emanate from underground, steamy geysers
Jet upward—there is no sky but weightless madness blends above.

Then, slowly, comes a rumble from the core until everything topples
And disintegrates into pieces of landscape, however rearranged,
However transformed by time, the features of demolition remain,
The end result of positive catastrophe, remnants of physical forces
Without plan but the eventual math of destiny, meaning, resource;
These are the effects, whatever ruptured them remains a mystery.

The Trespasser

Many busy themselves with obedience to authority,
blind and dumb, they sacrifice their best
to serve an implausible system;

precious are the hours
we sacrifice for wage,
that life is most rich
which has few dollars.

Why, flaunt insubordination,
you can do whatever you want to, live inviolate,
this may be deviant yet alternatively;

the program's power
to heal is obsolete,
they can not assuage
but make more grief.

I understand it's illegal, the purchase
of knowledge has always been,
that one must trespass in order to see the rewards;

but beyond the ledge
of private property,
lie the finest fruits
of all our industry.

They who articulate what is permissible do not own
the land they occupy, only pretend
to rule the rest with hired force and paper;

thus my foot is free
to walk wherever,
to observe the spoils
that others possess.

For a Country Girl

Bittersweet culminations of experience, inexplicable—
Serendipitous meetings of people ready to copulate—
Coordination, effort, appearance, success, age;
May these years bring exceptional circumstance
To light and pass through recurrent fevers unharmed.

Of this flesh, there is no finish, but a sumptuous
Overcoming of various instincts and fateful departures;
Where, I don't know, so attempt to express destiny
As one trembling on a stage voices soft objections
To the obvious convolution of all fading movement.

Some individuals will die, dramatic and unfulfilled—
Picture a capitulation to which most instants conform—
Yet the record shows perfection escapes everyone
As each frivolous rule breaks; humanity, once free,
Will perform spectacular stunts to impress the crowd.

Towards Tomorrow

"Marry me my Mississippi emblem
in a maze of overflowing stream,
in a rush of constant currents,
in a flood of momentous ease."

Below the waxing summer moon
a crowd gathers on levee lawn
to hear jazz music performed,
or else attend a baseball game.

Either way, the fireworks open
in multiple flowery explosions
and a train goes by with a hoot,
something impresses everyone.

Whether it's a festively lit bridge,
a boat gently bathing in the night
or an orange aura on the water,
everything impresses someone.

And the river's response was this:
"love does not cancel out love
but as blood, bleeds into blood
and all becomes one, a dream."

Pour The Foundation True

I stress nude contact
And the door opens to reveal a dimly lit room,
A sensual ride that links people together
in successive relations
And clothes fall to the floor.

The constant ability to touch one another
feels paramount,
There is just a mattress on the floor
And physical experience of love superlative,
knowledge plural,
Clairvoyant eyes that look familiar.

Intercourse overcomes death, sex confirms
We move in unison to achieve a picture
during real climax,
Drive toward bliss none can stop
Aware the beginning abuts the end,
Thus we grow closer to each other,
Assured that abstinence is futile by those
who crave orgasm
For blood is lava in their veins,
We who struggle with live temptation
And holy loin searing hormones pray
to reach the pinnacle,
To reciprocate bliss and lose consciousness.

Twin sufferers join in celebration,
Communicate power with automatic instinct,
mix the social cement,
Two fused into one alter destiny,
Aim at the attractive fulfillment of time.

Muse of Resentment

Beauty, youth and joy dissipate,
horror of death is our guide,
attempts at self possession fail,
inability mars perfection.

Dog, punishment, sin and need
picture us seeking lost ease,
a crazed predicament is amiss
on old fate, skip it, hang.

Who could do a lot of breeding
or massage out those dents,
fragile center of our tenderness,
a tortured, uneventful time.

That was just another disaster
conviction could not heal,
but cold, hardy souls around,
froze, dead of excitement.

I saw the carriage bar triumph
and lift kites of childhood,
weave material consecration
then fly off without bliss.

Spaces of order carved clouds
and laughs crumbled cells
in logical basements, music,
other names haze masks.

Perfect, solitary at well's edge,
ready to go plumb again
those senseless happy depths,
right without a question.

The Poisoned Well

And people came from miles around
To a metal pipe in the ground,
Small mouth of an artisan spring
That flowed into a shallow stream,
To fill plastic jugs with water—
With pure, fresh, delicious water.

Not everyone deemed it was wise
To sip straight from the specious well,
While most felt there could be no harm
Some thought better and made a test,
"Just so as to be sure," they said,
"Then maybe we will have a taste."

Who could have suspected the fields,
Those fertile, fertile, fertilized
Fields made the earth too saturate
With cancerous chemical salts,
An excess amount of nitrates—
Now few will dare to drink at all.

A Tornado

It happens a normal day
When wind mouths nothing in ears but routine,
as cattle gather on lush hill
To chew the grass of rural silence, people drive
to or from work
In nearby towns and further away,
A city candidates visit to solicit their votes.

Where cell phone towers poke the eyes of riders
(the guide wires outline concentric pyramids)
And riverboat casinos bring constant gambling,
Those who lose too much can ban themselves
from boarding an unlucky boat
Or better yet, get kicked off . . .

but the sky grows dark
It starts to rain, to pour, to thunderstorm
An eerie ambiance hovers over earth,
Violence shakes trees, haze grins on hills
A dark plate eclipses, proceeds to dip down in
a menacing manner,
Drops a fiendish finger from the clouds
And strikes and sucks and detonates all things.

There mows a volatile funnel of destruction
That throws trailer, car, pet, barn, fence
aluminum, concrete, whips
All debris and hail on hood and roof
Till someone gets hit and blood
soaks their fearful face,
They run for cover, traumatized by nature.

Some sit on their porch and sip refreshments
to television report
Or phone family members or tell strangers
what they possess,
Why they worry, the futility of flight altogether,
Others clamber down to the basement
Or leave their chair to look outside
nursing home windows
Or pray or freak or make love unaware.

Some do not leave their barstools for hours,
They listen to radio forecasts and grin,
Not knowing why they are glad.

A few do not fear the danger let loose,
They alone eschew disaster,
Shake a fist at demonic winds,
Scream volcanic epithets on high,
Taunt the twister with names,
Rail, call on havoc, court death.

Gone to wreck elsewhere,
It does not happen that negative judgment comes
like bad luck or witch's curse,
But because the world is wild
And we know too late.

The Angry Rider

Since the wind made me mad
  and dogs pursued my flesh,
I threw the damn reins down
  and let existence have it.

Lives

Gliding over the smooth clear surface
Of a lake between mountains,
Skimming through light bent within
    warm cool water,
Watching it reflect there,
Acts appeared before my eyes,
    a cinema of souls . . .

In a car, traveling down the highway
    to a restaurant, a couple
Argues about household arrangements,
Tend toward anger then silence.

Walking down the street, ambling after
    no certain place,
No particular bed or kitchen,
Not fully aware of the practicalities
    of city existence,
The poet wanders.

A group of people gathers in the park
    to listen to a concert,
A religious choir performs songs
    in foreign languages.

A policeman marks the crowd, aware
    there could be trouble,
His feet are tired, he will request time off.

A woman pushes a carriage with her just
    born baby inside,
She is proud and protective of her child
Who will become a diplomat.

Lying on the grass a young couple
    shares a bottle of wine,
They kiss and laugh as the world
    watches with envy.

A man on a bicycle shoots through
        traffic, narrowly avoids injury,
He does not stop but shudders at
        the thought of his extinction.

The weather anchor prepares to give
        her daily and weekly forecasts,
She is concerned with cloud coverage
        in the northeast of the country.

Two fisherman haul in their nets
        after a long days work,
They have caught more fish than in
        months, will rest tomorrow.

A bartender prepares for the night's
        work, he cuts citrus fruit
And lights candles, also notices
Winter coats on passersby.

The street sweeper curses his boss and
        local government for cutting
His hours, the pay is good,
He will sneak off for a long lunch
To drink beer with his mistress.

Schoolchildren gather outside the doors
        of their gymnasium, the game
Is with their biggest rival,
        firecrackers will get thrown
On the court, the game postponed.

A leery prostitute returns to the house
        of her abusive pimp,
She worries he will beat her again,
        worries he won't love her.

Electricians surround the fallen power
        line they are unable to fix,
Have called the company to shut down
        the entire block.

Rats in the sewer are on the move,
    flooding in the subways has
Caused them to migrate uptown
    in search of food and warmth.

The radio hangs from a hook above
    the Turkish man's hotdog stand,
He is out of chili and calls for his
    brother to hurry.

An Iraqi cab driver speeds through
    double parked cars, buses
And sails into the dark tunnel before
    turning on his headlights
And punching down the accelerator,
    he pumps the break, honks
And shakes his head as the car jolts
    to a stop at the tunnel's end.

A man with a gun in broad daylight
    shoots his landlord in the head
Then turns the gun on himself,
It is only after hours of negotiation
    and dozens of requests
On a radio station that he puts down
    the gun and allows himself
To be handcuffed.

A magazine stand ruffles in
    the harsh, cold wind,
Small bricks weigh down piles
    of today's newspaper.

The newest advertisement has gone up
    in the square, it is radical
In its appeal to people who can not
    afford to buy its objects.

A protest march has begun to demonstrate
    solidarity among minorities,
Thousands line the sidewalks to watch
    as people chant slogans.

The concert pianist cracks his knuckles
in anticipation of the performance,
He is nervous, remembers his mother's
advice upon leaving home.

The antiquarian society meets for its
three hundredth consecutive year,
Drinks are served and poetry read,
some dance after the reading.

A boy with a package of cigarettes
sits on a pile of rocks
Staring out over the river,
Contemplates his parents' divorce.

The chef recalls his native village
in the French countryside
And chokes back a tear, his father
has died in a farm accident.

Two brothers grasp hands and hug,
they have finished their first
Triathlon together, will celebrate
with the rest of their family.

The politician decides not to challenge
his adversary on the issue, his
Constituency is mainly concerned with
health care not abortion.

The train conductor yawns, his shift
will be over in one hour,
He hasn't slept in three days and
desperately wants sex.

The ship has reached the dock, men
tie her up and begin to unload
The thousands of crates of software,
a man in a suit signs the slip.

"I didn't come this far to back down
    now, not over this,"
The business executive thinks while
    staring out her office window.
The painter touches up his artwork
    and dreams of Florida,
He will stay away all winter if he
    can sell three more pieces.

And many more,
For as long as there are eyes to see
    the lives of people remain,
From a canoe one summer morning
I saw them play in a sunny lake,
Their acts in light and water.

Meditation on an Afterlife

Life will not end unless it fails to seek
permanent torch, ever anointing light,
or becomes nothing, and the elements
that made us flicker in and out of view,
illusions on parade, platinum ghosts;
wait, withdraw—liberation will come.

And we shall revel in reverse of death
without concern; walk through the doors
of an expensive mansion, find our way
down dark mirrored halls and roam
on fresh cut lawn, swim in the pool
or reunite with those we love the most.

Here's to existence beyond the threshold
of human knowledge, if not rich abode
then solitary aviation about the stars,
become one with heavenly magnitude,
engendered with wings, exploring suns—
for a spirit that survives the casket.

The Farmer

Who gives so much and gets so little in return
  as one who dies before his time
If such is possible, one who loses his life
  and family, land and legacy,
Whose reward for work is more work,
To grow more food, care for more animals
  and help more people
In the country he made productive,
Who but the farmer, whose name was father,
  son, husband, brother and friend?

If somehow still alive,
Would he do it all again,
Would he do it all the same?

Some think they know what it's like,
  how hard it is to survive,
How hard it is to make it through the day,
How hard it is to pass the night alone,
Although, it should be expected,
It's been decided that we live to die.

Water his grave with tears,
  sing litanies loud as thunder,
Demolish the church walls,
  burn the graveyard grass,
And scream, scream injustice.

But please forgive him for what he could not know;
Time has no purpose, God makes no promise,
Life has no end, even after death it stays
  with those who love,
Even when forgotten it continues on
In the acts of unsuspecting people,
In the physical celebrations of nature,
In the ongoing debate for social improvement,
In the spiritual transformation upon death,
In the phenomenal movement of matter, electricity,
  the eternal presence of shrouds.

Change to another set of clothes brother,
Those are covered in the cologne,
  of barn, field and garage,
They smell awful dirty and hang
  heavy on your limbs.

That decrepit costume is no longer useful,
Now the immortal suit of an afterlife
  or absolutely nothing,
Heaven, oblivion or reincarnation,
Flight to infinite possibility.

Yet who can be so accurate, who knows
  anything for certain,
Who can say what will happen,
None can, none can.

Anatomy of a Wave

The flight of geese across expansive territory;
parted clouds, intermittent *wa-enks* become
the occasion for much stopping of work,
the unusual formation I often notice,
that it is hardly a perfect letter V
rather like some broken imitation of V.
Still they weave their way through taller space
than any birds I've seen, stately Canadians.

Leaves Grow Back

Leaves grow back, fall through rigid limbs,
    become ashy cremations again.

Crisp droves litter pliant soil and compose
    pulpy layers like wet paper.

The rake claws and scratches at muck,
    failing to churn up feathers.

Empty are the outspread tree branches,
    open to light, palatial skeletons.

Vine entangled nerves wait to ooze color,
    to paint fresh fields in the air.

Leaves grow back, burst into view, float
    fluorescent roofs above us.

To a Critic

What good is soul,
Can it put a stop to suffering?

It is said we take refuge in lies
To continue a menial performance,
That we find beauty more than its effect
   and that one can level mountains,
Fill canyons, dam rivers, raise buildings
And still not learn the truth.

You are no different,
Your dreams are common and flash
   in deference to desire.

Riches and fame affect existence
   yet intimations abound,
I suppose more than anatomy,
Even greater, transcend thought,
An answer to our yearnings—
A work of spirit to please the body.

If love and death, joy and grief
   do not see us through
Then we must go beyond.

Change of Perspective

Back in the Midwest, country attire,
I look out upon the great plains with a promise
    in my chest,
To keep alive by intrigue or voice
The glorious presence of green imaginations.

I turn my back on history to face a certain
    sunrise over the East River,
To watch it dance upon the water,
To stay there and rest and dream reality.

"I've felt the surface of inhuman oceans
scratch the glass of other worlds,
smashed sand back into oblivion,
told many versions of a rural story,
and dictated reams that might happen."

Soon to stand beside the East River,
    near no small incubator,
Walking on sleek pavement,
Watching the fortunate go to work,
Not miniscule but colossal geometry guard
    an oblong island,
Emptiness braced, light on water
Brighten the bleary morning's promenade.

Traverse

Shrill medium, crawl out of mind,
harsh internal fluctuations
absolutely accentuate
the morbid, placid blackness
in which we sink.

It is not wholly impractical to be
diagnosed remote control,
to take pills for posy
when abysmal, drowning
before white banks.

Yesterday's comet dashed high,
fragments of helium fell
without suggestion,
agony, like spring weather
difficult to predict.

Good Morning Infidels

Unmoved by soldiers kicking down the door
I sit and look outside the window as my country
          undergoes invasion.

Of my three children, two died,
One was killed in the bombings, the other died
          resisting occupation
And soon my last will join her brothers.

Outraged by the presence of foreign troops,
Afraid for our lives, the integrity of our faith,
Together we prayed for the will to fight,
And Allah, the all merciful, obliged.

If it ever comes my turn to meet the enemy
          with brave suicide,
I, an aged poet, will put down the pen,
To write with a sword.

How many will sacrifice everything to be free
          from democracy's charade,
For the right to live a different way,
To govern without interference.

They have searched the house again,
Let them, what they seek is in my heart
And no interrogation will betray it,
For I fight, fight with legitimate conviction.

The Truck Stop

Furious commerce!
The bright lights and signs to the clouds
Where metal dinosaurs pause to refuel,
The constant growl of exhaust shakes
        the pavement sky,
Brakes squeal and nothing retires
        but sits in casual doom.

The volume of night,
When tired eyes and haggard faces ask
Who needs a job driving cross-country?
Who can stand the strain of driving away
        from everything familiar?

Such transportation tears people in half
And wrecks all sense of security.

I have seen the sunset on a summer evening,
Fallen under spells of gray and gold,
Seen soft explosions of purple and white
        and watched them disappear,
I know the slow silent feeling of home
        as it fades away.

But what the hell,
Why stay in places dust gathers?

When on the road,
Shooting to and from that orange ball,
Confronting the great enemy time,
        gunning down the line,
That long flat broken stripe,
I grow aware everything belongs.

Death of the Deer

It is bound to happen, the hunter looks forward
        to kill with patient anticipation,
After work he sharpens the blades of his arrow
        on a fine piece of stone, tests them
        by shaving hair from his arm,
After work he is not tired but more awake,
        he hasn't eaten, is hungry,
After work the hunter prepares his bow, bends
        it with all his strength so the string
        is tight, hard to pull and hold.

The road to the timber is gravel and dusty,
        the drive short,
The hike through the field is silent.

When the hunter enters nature he must respect it,
He walks amidst the pure solitude of trees
        lucky to live, fortunate to see,
Blessed with breath and subtle consciousness.

Still, he is inferior to animals,
He smells nothing, his instincts lapse,
He moves like a monkey and imitates to kill.
(Man is a poor beast were it not for brains
        and brutal intuition,
Without camouflage, he is obviously a predator.)
The hunter earns his way back into the wild
        by becoming it again,
Responsible for survival, he learns or starves,
Must match his will to the deer.

Hidden by a bunch of leaves, a trunk, a shadow
One with the woods, aloft, waiting and watching,
The hunter handles his weapon tenderly.

He envisions prey coming to the stage he has set,
        present yet absent,
Plays the deadly part of existence, lies ready
        to take nourishment from death,
To finger pounds of tension with stealthy hand,
To lift and draw with gentle arms, to position
        life within his sight.

The hunter aims for the deer with selfless love,
        takes the shot with care,
Receives the actual soul of the deer.
His ritual is holy, appreciation endless,
He shoots through the deer's heart
        with a cool razor shaft,
Feather and split tip exit fur and torn flesh,
Wounded, fallen, the deer lays dying
        on brown grass, steaming,
Its spirit loose, neck arched, head swivels
        round for one last look
And then collapses.

The hunter descends on the body of the deer
        with gratitude, touches its side
And feels nothing but his own pulse.

Autumn Purged

Hurt is always relevant,
we agonize for fun and claim speed
    our day's objective.

The few who still care for life want
    comfort not depravity,
there's already enough misery
    and depression to exit.

It's good to go, take hold of light
    and switch with haste,
flick the plastic tip of time on,
free energy from hidden reserve.

  Let others shoulder argument
    and bare religious boulder,
  they grapple with decadence,
    meander, savor the least.

And in this ritual be immersed;
    wash with resilience,
none of the quality is gone,
    dignity thrives, virtue lives.

                Across threshold
of unimagined terrain-sculpted myth,
different perceptions persist,
    release the furniture!

Welcome Apparitions

With what incredible sense,
extraordinary ability to perceive,
alarming alacrity, does one
recognize omnipresent companions?

Definite signs suggest
an ongoing convergence of strangers,
the revelation in discussion
and clear exaltation of friendship.

Indomitable is that spirit
against all kinds of antagonists,
who gathers numerous allies
for miraculous events will ensue.

Peripheral powers visit
with increasing coincidence,
each phenomenal detail of life
makes laughter more momentous.

The Ballad of Filth

An incorporeal presence, malodorous
  Decomposition, became music,
ascendant fumes defiantly crawled up
  heaps of slime, muck evolved.

Rode through polluted tunnels,
found fresh voyage in common silt—
  tar pit, hog lot, train stop
produced fossil, meat and mobility.

Oil fuels this microcosmic world
  born of mud, made of clay,
clings desperately to cleanliness—
  rain on rocks and waterfalls.

Brown is the hue, even better black
  from which all others derive;
aboriginal unknown, a multiverse—
  first, profuse, radiant night.

Assume wild initial conditions,
credit pyrotechnics with creation
  yet know labor precedes
moments of lightning like insight.

When in scientific sludge we try
  to inhale the upper crust
with imperfect effect, recall
  we once slid out of the soil.

Where the Tree Falls

Neither side of the fence was our land
Yet we needed the wood for fuel,
Thus performed a favor for the rancher,
Whose horse or cattle could get out
Come spring, and the farmer, whose crop
Would crush when the still standing half
Of the old dead tree finally collapsed.

We drove through deep, snowy pasture
To reach the fallen half, sawed it up
And loaded various logs on the truck,
Then cut down the rest of the tree
Which, timber, crashed into the field
On the other side of the fence, limbs
Lay all over as evidence of our work.

Although it was by design that the tree
Should fall over the fence, so as not
To hit in some thorny brush or shear
The barbed wire fence, even so, we had
To travel 'round the entire length and
Across a pathless plain of uneven earth,
No small task for one morning's work.

And when we had done what we'd set out
To do, gathered up kindling, and rode
Back home to chop our pile of wood,
So it could burn inside an iron stove
And heat the house that keeps us warm
All winter long, we unloaded, then split
The booty into slivered pieces with an axe.

The Best Alive

When you came to the city
we rendezvoused at a bar,
you wore college colors
and accepted my praise
like a sincere actress.

Come back, come back
fair one come back;
I cannot go with you yet.

Favorite muse is too subtle
a phrase, surreptitious,
we went to *La Bohème*
and the moment lives
eternal. I will revel
in it with you forever
perched on the third ring.

Come back, come back
dear one come back;
the things I cannot forget.

You are an opera whose
music fills my ears
with bittersweet applause,
self sounding, that none
can produce save you,
absolute to my soul.

Come back, come back
good one come back;
I cannot go where you go.

Mate, love, mistress, master;
we are none to each other,
free from care, have separate,
unconnected lives,
even so my heart crowned
you queen of amour.

Come back, come back
fair one come back;
the peace you will know.

We ate Moroccan, Spanish
and spoke of plans
walking through the park—
infinite lights, one sparked
your eye, spirited one,
the essence of the universe
appeared to condense
the best alive within you.

Come back, come back
dear one come back;
I cannot go with you yet.

If you stood by a window
the world would end
in happiness, your body
a brilliant female statue;
beauty you possess,
charm is your voice,
grace your calling,
poise when reflection hits.

Come back, come back
good one come back;
the things I cannot forget.

Perfect, true, no, are words
elegant, wild, too dull
to speak of your visage,
many call me liar
yet I don't exaggerate,
no man or woman could
persuade me otherwise.

Come back, come back
fair one come back,
I cannot go where you go.

Peconic Bay

If on good ground this life should fail to be,
let it return to the grand Peconic
to rest one knee in water, one on land,
conjoin a salty accession of swells
with swollen eyes and lips and kiss a calm
yet otherworldly, wet, enveloping
warm sense of vulvic power unforeseen.

Sorrow overruled, mortal mania
no longer lingering like mean perfume;
a volatile broken body redeemed
on dappled shore and transparent bay,
aquatic scope encircled by vast range,
the wind careens into a sloping bluff
and sends sand avalanching to the beach.

Untitled

Hail the daybreak—
When sunlight sings on the waters
  of the earth,
When birds win their way
  through wind,
When bodies wake to the mystery
  inherent in all things,
When life begins anew!

Hail birth and death—
They define us, we are morning
  and subsequent night,
They fly as gull and crow,
They blaze outside windows,
They are moon and land of dreams,
  blinding black of sleep.

Hail the place and current situation,
  real and foreknowledge,
That which transcends reason,
That being I do not understand yet
  entirely believe in,
That offers everything at once,
That fulfills all longing.

More essential fiction from Vagabond Press

Déjà Vu
Richard Kendrick

ISBN 0-9755716-0-5
352 pages
$15.00 (paper)

If ordering directly from Vagabond Press, add $3 postage and handling per order.

VAGABOND PRESS
PO Box 4830
Austin, TX 78765
vagabondpress.com

Alden Homer and Blake Whitman are traveling their own paths, which seem to cross more frequently than usual for a couple of dissimilar guys on the road in Asia. Their thoughts and experiences are pieces of a puzzle that the reader can assemble, as this seminal work allows the reader to participate in the construction of the narrative.

Alden, who experimented with drugs during his Ivy League days, is now in his 50s. He has passed through Wall Street and sacrificed a marriage to his literary aspirations. Searching for the Muse, he'll settle for enlightenment. Blake is taking a year off before medical school, and is enthusiastically seeking the adventure he could only read about—or see in the movies—back home in Middle America. He chases the Exotic. Independently or together, these two colorful characters encounter a nymphomaniac, a murder victim, Christian fundamentalists, Hindu holy men, inmates at a mental institution, and a yeti - not to mention their own dreams.

DÉJÀ VU, Richard Kendrick **ISBN-10**: 0-9755716-0-5
353 pages $15 **ISBN-13:** 978-0-9755716-0-6

. . . full of lyrical descriptions of far off lands yet hits home with absolute poignance; it presents the world in a prism of adventure and experimentation, so much so that it reminds one of the enduring spirit of American literature. Kendrick revives Melville, Twain, and Kerouac in a voice that openly rejects the conventions of today, even as it demands fresh perspective. The book is essentially a search for truth; its form is unique and inventive, based upon the cyclical nature of time, subjectivity and the concept of fulfillment. I recommend it to everyone tired of the monotony of an everyday performance without avail, to you who lust for travel! -- *Lucas Hunt*

A rare book that combines modernist formal experimentation with excellent post-modernist content and prose; this novel is as much about form as it is about plot. Part *bildungsroman* part travelogue, both funny and serious, a blend of facts, fictions, and dreams; Déjà Vu . . . risks comparison with novels like Cortázar's *Hopscotch* and Perec's *Life: a User's Manual* (I generally don't like to use the word "risk" in art criticism, but I think it's appropriate here) and I think it stands up very well. Saying that I actually preferred this to either of them would sound pretentious; but . . . the content of this novel is more to my liking than that of the others. -- *Rick Russo*

CODE GREEN, Greg Jenkins **ISBN-10:** 0-9755716-1-3
227 pages $15 **ISBN-13:** 978-0-9755716-1-3

Chip Stone is a male nurse who works in a psychiatric hospital and has almost as many behavioral issues as the residents he cares for. These include DeWitt, a cultural critic gone bonkers; Tim Valentine, who snacks on light bulbs; Philip Nolan, who contends (correctly) that he's a character in a book; and Glinda Moon, an anorexic witch. As the violence at his workplace intensifies, the confused Stone sets out on a desperate but comical odyssey to find his estranged wife–and himself. His wanderings take him through a twisted netherworld where he meets old friends, new enemies and one highly unusual sister-in-law. He discovers that the line between the sane and the not-so-sane is more gossamer than even he had suspected. With over-the-top characters and gaudy, entertaining prose, this engaging work offers a bumptious blend of humor and pathos well-suited to the uncertainties of the new millennium.

THE ROOM WITH CLOSETS, A. Pablo Iannone **ISBN-10:** 0-9755716-3-X
107 pages $10 **ISBN-13:** 978-0-9755716-3-7

These short stories–tied together by common threads–travel the literary landscape from grim political reality to joyous flights of fantasy and humor. Join José Conti, his extended family, and his friends to obtain more insight about life, love, and human nature. There is Margarita, and the comical reminders of death that greet her on the morning of her honeymoon; a Spanish shepherd who changes identities in order to sail to America; and three Argentines suffering the nightmare of trying to obtain a passport from their fascist government. There is the room with closets, and its locked door that mysteriously opens by itself; a youth who hijacks a moto-copter, seeing the "Virgin of Carmen" during his flight; and a student of quantum physics and member of the underground, who discovers how to cheat death (but not life).

If ordering directly from Vagabond Press, add $3 postage and handling per order.
Vagabond Press, PO Box 4830, Austin, TX 78765